A peacock IN THE LAND OF PENGUINS

A peacock IN THE LAND OF PENGUINS

A Tale of Diversity and Discovery

**Barbara "BJ" Hateley
and Warren H. Schmidt**

Illustrations by Sam Weiss
Foreword by Ken Blanchard

Berrett-Koehler Publishers
San Francisco

Berrett-Koehler Publishers, Inc.
155 Montgomery Street
San Francisco, CA 94104-4109
Tel: 415-288-0260   Fax: 415-362-2512

ORDERING INFORMATION

Individual sales. Berrett-Koehler publications are available through most bookstores. They can also be ordered direct from Berrett-Koehler at the address above.

Quantity sales. Special discounts are available on quantity purchases by corporations, associations, and others. For details, contact the "Special Sales Department" at the Berrett-Koehler address above.

Orders for college textbook/course adoption use. Please contact Berrett-Koehler Publishers at the address above.

Orders by U.S. trade bookstores and wholesalers. Please contact Publishers Group West, 4065 Hollis Street, Box 8843, Emeryville, CA 94662. Tel: 510-658-3453; 1-800-788-3125. Fax: 510-658-1834.

Printed in the United States of America

Printed on acid-free and recycled paper that meets or exceeds the strictest state and U.S. guidelines for recycled paper (85% recycled, including 15% post-consumer waste).

Library of Congress Cataloging-in-Publication Data

Hateley, B.J. (Barbara J.)
   A peacock in the Land of Penguins; a tale of diversity and
discovery/by Barbara "BJ" Hateley and Warren H. Schmidt;
illustrations by Sam Weiss; foreword by Ken Blanchard. — 1st ed.
      p. cm.
   ISBN 1-881052-71-0 (pbk.: acid-free paper)
   1. Pluralism (Social sciences) — Fiction. 2. Fables. I. Schmidt,
Warren H. II. Title.
   PS3558.A7378P43 1994
   813'.54–dc20   94-24531
                                                            CIP

First Edition
99 98 97 96 95   10 9 8 7 6 5 4 3 2

Cover and book design: Vinje Design, Inc., San Francisco, CA

We dedicate this book

to all who yearn to fly free

and show their true colors —

and to all who have the wisdom to learn

from those who are different.

Foreword

Every once in a while a small book comes along that deals with a profound subject in a very simple, elegant way. *A Peacock in the Land of Penguins* is such a book. It brings new insight into the much-discussed issue of diversity in the workplace – and it does so in a most engaging manner. Through the medium of a fable, this book helps us to see what can happen when we try to express ourselves fully and courageously in an environment created by executives and managers who view the world very differently.

This is the story of Perry the Peacock – a bright, talented, colorful bird – who comes to live in the Land of Penguins. He soon runs into problems because the penguins have established a chilly organizational climate that is formal, bureaucratic, and governed by a vast array of written and unwritten rules. Although his talent is recognized, his different and unusual style makes the penguins feel uneasy. His experience reflects that of "birds of a different feather" in many of today's organizations. While the gospel of "valuing diversity" is preached in seminars and meeting rooms throughout American business, government, education, and religious institutions, the rhetoric does not always match the reality.

Being "different" is much more than a matter of race and gender. Diversity in its fullest sense involves a broad range of human uniqueness – personality, work style, perception and attitudes, values and lifestyle, work ethic, world view, communication style, and much more. Valuing diversity means appreciating and encouraging people to be who they really are, helping them to develop their full potential, and utilizing their special talents, skills, ideas, and creativity.

This delightful corporate fable, based on the experiences of real people, follows the adventures of Perry the Peacock and other exotic birds as they

try to make their way in the Land of Penguins.
Their story is both entertaining and enlightening.
This is a tale of the perils and possibilities of being
"different" in a world that values comfort, safety,
and the predictability of conformity.

Anyone involved in an organization – executives,
human resource people, managers and supervisors,
and employees – should read this little book. There
are important insights for all of us!

Ken Blanchard

Acknowledgments

This book reflects the creative thoughts of many minds and the encouragement of many hearts. This page mentions only a few of those to whom we owe so much . . .

First and foremost, we wish to thank Margret McBride, without whose early and continued support, encouragement, and editorial suggestions this book would not have been completed. We are deeply grateful for her guidance throughout every step of the creative process.

Steven Piersanti, our publisher, is very much a kindred spirit and a joy to work with. It has indeed been a creative partnership, and his thoughtful suggestions helped us to refine and polish our work. Steve and his team at Berrett-Koehler have invested much time and energy in helping us get our story into final format. We look forward to continued collaboration and a fruitful future.

And Sam Weiss, who turned out to be much more than an illustrator, helped bring our characters to life. In the process, he enriched our project with his thoughtful insights, questions, and comments. We appreciate the way his own "peacock" nature shines through his drawings!

We also wish to thank the real-life "exotic birds," as well as the "penguins," whose experiences inspired our corporate fable. They will undoubtedly recognize themselves and the roles they played in the Land of Penguins. Extra thank-you's go to Phyllis Pfeiffer, Jim Shaffer, Larry Strutton, and Jeff Hall, whose inspiration, critiques, and feedback were especially helpful.

And finally, a very special thanks to our families, especially Reggie Schmidt, Michael Hateley and Gloria Gallagher, who provided continuous support, encouragement, and helpful critiques as our fable took shape. Their love and attention nurtures our creative spirits.

BJH & WHS

There once was a time,
in the not so distant past,
when penguins ruled many lands
in the Sea of Organizations.

These penguins were not always wise,
they were not always popular,
but they were always in charge.

Most organizations looked the same:

Top executives
and managers
wore their distinctive penguin suits,
while worker birds
of many kinds
wore colors and outfits
that reflected their work
and their lifestyles.

Birds who aspired to move up
in their organizations
were encouraged to become
as penguin-like as possible —
to shorten their steps
and learn the penguin stride,
to wear penguin suits,
and follow
the example of their leaders.

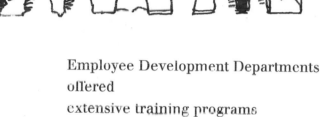

Employee Development Departments
offered
extensive training programs
on
appropriate penguin-like behavior.

The rules
and norms
were clear
from Day One.

Penguins advised in subtle
(and not so subtle) ways:

"This is the way we do things here."

"If you want to be successful,
be like us."

Some of the birds
who wanted to move up
in the pecking order
became very good
at taking on the penguin look
and penguin behaviors.

But even *they*
found that
they never quite
made it
into key positions.

It was assumed by all
that penguins
were natural leaders —
orderly, loyal, and good team players.

Penguins could be trusted
to put
the organization's interests
ahead
of personal and family concerns.

Other birds
were thought to be
more flighty
and less dependable.

Of course,
this was never stated
out loud
or in writing.

Because,
like every organization,
penguins wanted to be seen
as fair-minded and
ready to promote
on the basis of
talent,
hard work,
and contribution.

But everyone really knew —

The penguins
had always been in charge,
and
the penguins
***would** always be in charge.*

The elder penguins
would take
younger penguins
under their wings
and coach them
on
how to be successful.

They would invite them
to play golf
and go jogging.

They would sit together
in the executive dining room
and talk about sports.

It was clear to everyone
who the important penguins were.

It was also clear
that the penguins
felt most comfortable
around each other.

Life was harmonious
in the Land of Penguins,
as long as everyone played
by the penguins' rules.

The other birds
in the organization
knew how to act
to make the penguins
feel comfortable
and secure.

But there came a time
when things began to change
in the Land of Penguins . . .

Senior penguins
would visit
other lands,
where they encountered
interesting birds
who impressed them
with their
management talent,
experience,
and accomplishments.

"These birds are not penguins,"
the elders thought,
"but perhaps
they could become penguins
if we brought them to our land
and trained them
in our penguin ways."

"Surely
these impressive and unusual birds
could adapt to life
in the Land of Penguins,
and the talent
they bring
would make us
even more successful."

"Our climate is different —
chilly and cold.
And our terrain is unique —
icy and barren.

"But we have thrived there
and so perhaps
will these new birds.

"If they are as smart
as we think they are,
they can adjust
to our weather and our ways."

And this was how
Perry the Peacock
came to live
in the Land of Penguins . . .

Now
Perry was clearly
not a penguin.

In fact,
he was the antithesis of penguinity —

Perry was a peacock —
a bright, colorful, and noisy bird.

Perry was a very talented peacock,
who had accomplished
some very impressive things
in his own land.

He could write well
and was excellent
at managing his budgets.
He was creative and imaginative,
and at the same time,
practical and sensible.

He had many friends and admirers
in his own land,
and was very popular and well-liked.

Senior managers
in the Land of Penguins
were intrigued
when they met Perry the Peacock.

They knew that he was different —
but they were impressed
with what he had achieved in his career,
and they were fascinated
with the possibilities
that he represented.

They felt that Perry
had real Penguin Potential.

Perry, in turn,
was attracted to the penguins
because of the great things
he had heard and read
about their land —
the promise of status,
and wealth,
and a sense of belonging
to a great and powerful enterprise.

It was a rich land —
and all the birds
were paid extremely well.

"My future will be brighter,"
he thought,
"in this new land."

And so the penguins
and the peacock
agreed.

He would join them,
and together
they would achieve
great things.

At first
everyone was delighted.

The penguins were pleased
and impressed
with their new recruit.

He stood out
from the crowd
in the way he sparkled
and displayed flashes of color
every now and then.

And Perry was pleased, too,
with the novelty
and the newness.

He was impressed
by the penguins —
they looked so important
in their black and white suits,
especially
when they gathered together
for meetings
and company events.

Their formality and manners
were so different
from anything
he had ever seen
or experienced
before.

Now the peacock
was careful
in the beginning
not to display
too much of his colorful nature.

You see, some friends
in his own land
had warned Perry about penguins —

They had cautioned him
about the rules
and the style
with which the penguins
governed their land.

So he kept his feathers
folded up
much of the time,
and would only occasionally
flash them open
to dazzle the penguins
with the full range of his talent and color.

He wanted
to be taken seriously
and he wanted
to be successful.

So he subdued
his own peacock nature
for a while,
until he could be sure
that the penguins had accepted him
completely.

He was confident
that when he produced
good results for them,
they would embrace him fully —
in all his peacock glory —
and he could relax
and just be himself.

You see,
things were very different
in the land where he had grown up —
in the Land of Learning.

In the Land of Learning
there were LOTS of different kinds of birds.

There were wise birds (owls),
and powerful birds (eagles),
and hunting birds (hawks),
improbable birds (ostriches),
elegant birds (swans),
and awkward birds (gooney birds).

It was crowded and noisy,
with a buzz of activity
and the rough and tumble
of competition.

Birds had to work hard,
learn fast,
and live by their wits
and creativity
in order to be successful.

It was an exhilarating
but tough
environment!

The motto in the Land of Learning was:

All the birds
worked hard
to prove their talent
and earn their place
in the sun.

In the Land of Learning
the birds didn't always
get along peaceably.

Sometimes there were
conflicts and differences,
struggles and irritations.

But conflicts and differences
were valued
because the birds believed
that that's how new ideas get tested.

Discussion,
debate,
and argument —
that's the way
change was introduced
and progress was made.

Nobody cared
if you were a penguin or a peacock,
a dove or a bluejay.

Being smart
and talented
and productive
was all that mattered.

Initiative,
creativity,
and results
were most highly prized.

It was what was inside you
and what you contributed
that counted —
not the kind or color
of feathers you wore.

But Perry the Peacock
was in for
some very different challenges
when he left
the Land of Learning
and went to work
in the Land of Penguins.

He was used to hard work
and fighting for his ideas
and competing with
many different kinds of birds.
But nothing in his background
had prepared him for
the unique ways
and special customs
of the Land of Penguins.

He wanted to do well
and be successful.

He was flattered
that these powerful and prestigious penguins
had recruited him
into their ranks,
and he wanted to please them.

He studied the penguins' walk,
their talk,
and their style.

"How strange,"
he thought to himself,
"they all look alike.
They're like clones of each other."

He was intrigued
and puzzled
at the same time.

And as time went on, his troubles began . . .

Some of the penguins
began to grumble
that his distinctive peacock voice
was too loud.

You see,
penguins speak
in very subdued,
modulated
tones,
and the peacock's laughter
and excited exclamations
startled their time-honored
sense of propriety.

His feathers began to show
more and more all the time,
as he worked hard
and accomplished
many great things.

Everyone agreed
that he was quite talented
and productive,
and they liked the impressive results
of his work.

But his flashy, colorful style
made some
of the senior penguins
uneasy.

Many of the other penguins
in the land
were delighted
with this new and unusual bird
in their midst.

They called him
"a breath of fresh air"
and welcomed his exuberance.

Some of the junior penguins
privately speculated
about how long he would last
in the Land of Penguins.
They saw
how un-penguinlike he was,
and wondered how long
this would be tolerated by the
elders.

A couple of the senior penguins
  tried to take him
  under their wings and coach him.

"Look," they said,
"we like your work,
  but some of the elders
  are uncomfortable with your style."

"You need to change to be accepted here."

"Why don't you put on a penguin suit,
  so you look more like us?"

"It doesn't fit,"
responded Perry the Peacock.

"It's too tight and constraining.
My tail feathers will get crushed
and my wings can't move well."

"I can't work if I'm not comfortable."

The elders said,
"Well then,
maybe you could paint your feathers
black and white,
like ours."

"Then at least
you wouldn't look
quite so different."

"What's wrong with the way I am?"
Perry asked.

He was hurt and confused.

"I work hard,
I produce great results —
everyone says so."

"Why can't you look at my work
rather than my feathers?"

"Aren't my accomplishments
more important
than my style?"

"It's such a small thing,"
the penguins responded.

"You are smart and talented.
You could have a bright future here.
You just need to act
more like us
and then
the elders will be more comfortable."

"You need to wear a penguin suit,
and soften your voice,
and shorten your steps."

"Just watch all the other penguins —
see how they act?"

"Try to be like the rest of us."

Perry believed
that their intentions were good,
but their words wounded him nonetheless.

"Why can't I just be who I am?
Why do I have to change
to be accepted by you?"
he asked.

"That's just the way things are here,"
the penguins shrugged.

"It's the same everywhere
in the Sea of Organizations."

He suspected they might be right,
but his heart didn't want to accept it.

He thanked them
for their words of advice
and their concern for him,
and he went back to his nest
to think things over.

As the months rolled by,
he discussed his dilemma
with some of the other birds he trusted.

Several of them
were also new birds
who had been recruited
around the same time as
Perry's arrival
in the Land of Penguins.

Many of them
were experiencing
similar kinds
of problems . . .

Edward the Eagle
complained that he, too,
was getting pressure
to change.

He was smart and powerful
and very skilled at his work,
and he even wore the requisite penguin suit.

But Edward didn't talk
or act like a penguin,
and this bothered the elders.

They were embarrassed
by his accent,
and sent him to
a prestigious,
tradition-steeped
Eastern Business School
for special executive penguin training.

But it didn't work —
he was still an eagle in penguin's clothing.

He couldn't change who he was.

And Helen the Hawk
had similar problems.

She was beautiful and powerful —
smart, sharp, and aggressive.
She was a skilled hunter,
with fierce competitive instincts.

She wore her penguin suit,
occasionally more colorful
than the male penguins,
but still acceptable.

Helen tried to adapt
to the style of the penguins,
but her hawk-like nature
would always reveal itself.

Her talons were sharp,
her eyes piercing,
her manner intense,
her hunter's instincts
ever alert.

And her aggressive style
made the elders very uncomfortable.

It was the same story
with Mike the Mockingbird.

He was an especially brilliant bird —
creative,
imaginative,
and impulsive.
He was attracted by sparkling ideas.

He flew fast,
worked hard,
and jumped around
making good things happen
all over the Land of Penguins.

But Mike soon discovered that
penguins are territorial birds,
who build their empires,
establish their pecking order,
and fiercely resent anyone
who comes into their turf
without being properly invited.

Since Mike was not a penguin,
he was not sensitive
to the politics
and the turf issues
of the senior penguins.

With his penchant for creativity
and imagining possibilities
outside the ordinary,
he sometimes offended
some of the elders
by flying into their territories.

They were threatened and annoyed
at his intrusions.

Like Edward the Eagle
and Helen the Hawk,
Mike wore his penguin suit
and tried his best
to learn the ways of the penguins
so he would be accepted by them.

But ultimately,
he could not change who he really was.

The story was similar
with Sara the Swan.

She was an optimistic dreamer,
with unusual visions
for the future
of the Land of Penguins.

She had interesting ideas,
unique ideas,
good ideas —

but her ideas
often were not heard
because she expressed them
in such a gentle way.

Her style was graceful,
her manner gracious,
but the penguins
had doubts about
her toughness
and her strength.

There were others as well . . .

The thing they all had in common
was that none of them
had grown up
in the Land of Penguins.

They had been
recruited and hired
from other places.

The penguin elders
had enticed these outsiders
with promises of success:

"We want your fresh thinking
and new ideas.
We admire your track record
and want you to do
great things for us."

But
as soon as the new birds
were inside the organization,
the elders issued them
penguin suits
and began pressuring them
to talk,
act,
and think
more like penguins.

The penguins said,
"We value diversity."

But their actions said otherwise.

As the exotic new birds
discussed
their mutual frustrations
among themselves,
they tried
to figure out
what to do.

Several of them
decided to try
to change the culture
rather than
let the culture change them.

"We'll work on our bosses,
and other key penguins,"
they vowed,
"without
being too obvious,
of course."

They each
developed strategies
for becoming
Agents of Change
within the Land of Penguins.

Edward the Eagle
adopted a **"Strategy of Support."**

*"Catch your boss
doing something right . . .
(or approximately right!)"*

Whenever his boss
accepted
any new idea,
Edward would reinforce him
by saying,
"I appreciate
your willingness
to try
something different.
Your support
makes my job
interesting
and rewarding."

Helen the Hawk
had her own ideas
about how to bring about change.
She used a **"Strategy of Hopeful Thinking."**

> *"Act on the basis*
> *of assumptions*
> *you'd **like** to be true . . .*
> *(with caution, of course!)"*

Helen would regularly send
her boss
newspaper clippings
and magazine articles
with a personal note
which read:

"Because
of your continuing interest
in learning new ways
to handle our marketing,
I thought
you'd like to see
the attached article
about
Prosperous Enterprise, Inc.
in the recent issue of
the 'Journal of Successful Organizations.'"

Mike the Mockingbird
decided he would try
an extremely bold strategy —
a **"Strategy of Calculated Ignorance."**

"Violate
penguin policy —
and if caught —
use the Puzzled Prodigal Response."

Whenever Mike was questioned
about making a particular decision,
he would assume
an expression of puzzlement
as he described
how a shortcut
would achieve something
that everyone
had agreed
was important.

Sara the Swan,
being much gentler
in her approach,
tried a *"Strategy of Safe Learning."*

*"Expose
the Senior Penguins
to new ideas
in settings
where
they won't be embarrassed
by having to respond."*

Sara would casually mention
her ideas and suggestions
in quiet conversations
and informal settings.

She "planted ideas,"
nurtured them slowly,
and watched for progress.

Some of the other birds —
who were determined
to transform themselves —
tried very hard
to become penguins.

They walked the penguin walk;
they talked the penguin talk.

They preened
and practiced
to produce the desired result.

But ultimately they failed,
because
they couldn't change
who they really were.

And a few birds,
like Perry,
didn't even try
to become penguins.

Perry just knew
in his heart
that there must be
at least *one* land in
the vast Sea of Organizations
where
he could be a peacock
and be valued
for his uniqueness.

He resisted
the penguins' advice and pressure,
firm in his conviction
that he should be valued
for his results.

Over time,
things got worse
for Perry
and the other exotic birds
in the Land of Penguins . . .

Their strategies
to change
the penguin way of doing things
met with
resistance and red tape.

Their ideas and efforts
were discounted
and dismissed.

Their questions of "Why?"
were answered with:
"This is the way
we've *always* done things here."

The exotic birds learned
through painful experience
that the culture
of the land
was deeply entrenched.

The structures and systems
were rigid and unbending.
Policies and procedures
ensured the continuity
of the penguin practices.

It eventually became clear
that individual efforts
at persuasion and influence
were foolish and futile
in the face of such
longstanding tradition
and structure.

The exotic birds realized
that the penguin ways
had developed
over many years
and would not change
easily or soon.

Their strategies
to change themselves
also fell short,
because
deep down inside
they just weren't penguins.

*They couldn't change
who they really were.*

Their hearts were filled
with frustration,
disappointment,
and sadness.

They had come
to the Land of Penguins .
with such high hopes
and great expectations.

They had wanted to contribute
and be successful.

But what they got instead
was quiet criticism,
stifling conformity,
and subtle rejection.

And so,
one by one,
Perry and the other new birds
each began to realize
the same thing —

*They could not be themselves
in the Land of Penguins.*

They had to move on.

They knew their futures
lay somewhere else
in the vast Sea of Organizations.

Some of the new birds
left the Land of Penguins
on their own.

Others
were pushed out
by the senior penguins,
who said,
"You make us too uncomfortable.
You don't fit here.
You must leave."

Whether they left on their own
or were forced out by the elders,
all the departing birds
shared one thing in common —
the pain and confusion
of being different,
and the sadness
and disappointment
of not being accepted for who they were.

These birds of a different feather
had all struggled
with the same dilemma:

How much
could they
or would they
change to "fit in"
and be accepted
in the Land of Penguins,
and how much
could they be themselves?

What price would they pay to be successful?

And the penguins had their own dilemma:

How much diversity
could they tolerate in their land
and still maintain
their own comfort level?

Wouldn't
all these differences
endanger
their harmonious corporate culture?

The penguins,
after all,
had enjoyed
many years of profitable success
by following
historic penguin traditions
and ways of doing business.

They were reluctant
to change the style
that had made them great.

And they were disappointed
that so many
of their new recruits
did not work out.

Perry the Peacock
was the first to leave.

He had many friends
from other lands,
and they told him
of a new and wondrous place
they had visited in their travels.

They described it as
"the Land of Opportunity."

There,
they told him,
his work
and his contributions
would be valued —
and his uniqueness
would be applauded,
not criticized.

He could be
colorful,
flamboyant,
and enthusiastic,
and others would appreciate him
for his distinctive style.

Dare he hope
that these reports were true?

Was this the place
he had longed for?

He had to go
and see for himself.

When Perry arrived in
the Land of Opportunity
he found that it
was totally different
from the Land of Penguins . . .

Here,
workers and bosses
didn't waste
time and energy
pretending to be
something different
from what they were.

They knew
that they needed
many different kinds of birds
in order to thrive
in the turbulent and competitive
Sea of Organizations.

And they knew that
the most important requirement
for organizational success
is acceptance and trust.

It is acceptance and trust
that make it possible
for each bird
to sing its own song —
confident that it will be heard —
even by those
who sing with a different voice.

All the birds
expressed themselves freely,
and their lively exchanges
of differing views
ensured
that their work
and their ways
were constantly improving.

Best of all,
they had confidence
in their leaders,
birds of many kinds
who had risen to
their positions
through talent,
skill,
and ability.

The motto here was:

E PLURIBUS MAXIMUS
(Greatness from Many)

Some birds swam,
many flew,
and some kept their feet
planted firmly on the ground.

This gave them
many different perspectives
on the world —
which they shared
easily and openly
with one another.

Their shared knowledge made them wise.
And their wisdom made them successful.

Perry knew
he had found his new home.

As the months and years
rolled by,
one by one,
Edward the Eagle,
Helen the Hawk,
Mike the Mockingbird,
and Sara the Swan
also made their way
to the Land of Opportunity.

They had heard from Perry
about the freedom
and openness
that existed there.

In this land,
Edward could fly free and high,
soaring as fast
as his wings could carry him.

Others admired
his grace and power —
and commented
on what an inspiration he was
to younger birds
who came from humble beginnings
but had ambitious dreams
of flying high someday themselves.

Nobody even noticed
the way he spoke,
with his unique accent.

Helen,
who had rattled the penguins
with her intensity
and her keen competitive instincts,
found a place
where she was welcome
in the Land of Opportunity.

Her colleagues
valued her hunting skills
and her ability to spot
changing trends
and possibilities
for new ventures.

They commented frequently
on her elegant beauty
and distinctive style.

She was perfectly suited
for her new position
in the Land of Opportunity.

Mike
at long last
experienced the creative joy
of jumping from project to project,
working hard and fast,
and stirring up new ideas
wherever he went.

No longer fettered
by a rigid pecking order
and boundaries
dictated by penguins,
his productivity skyrocketed —
and others marveled
at his amazing skills.

Sara, too,
found the Land of Opportunity
to be a hospitable place
for her dreamy,
reflective,
imaginative
style of working.

She started writing
and pursuing ideas
in ways
she once thought
would never be possible
in a place of work.

Other birds flocked to her,
wanting to work with her
and share
in the realization
of her dreams.

She was appreciated
for the freedom
she allowed others,
and
for her gentle style.

These diverse birds
all prospered and grew
as never before.

They felt affirmed
and appreciated
by the other birds
in the land.

They experienced a new freedom,
allowing them to fly,
each with their own unique style.

They worked hard —
and enjoyed
the fruits of their labors.

*A*bove all else,
they knew the joy of just being themselves.

Perry the Peacock flashed his colorful feathers;

Edward the Eagle soared with power and grace;

Helen the Hawk skillfully kept watch and hunted;

Mike the Mockingbird followed his creative instincts and innovative ideas; and

Sara the Swan drifted and floated with the currents.

Perry and his friends
found that
life was good and
their future was bright
in the Land of Opportunity.

There
they could all succeed —
each with a different style —
and make contributions
that would be welcomed and appreciated
by their colleagues
and coworkers.

They came to realize
that the Land of Opportunity
is more than a place . . .

It is a state of mind.

The Land of Opportunity is an attitude.

It is
an openness to new ideas,
a willingness to listen,
an eagerness to learn,
a desire to grow,
and the flexibility to change.

The Land of Opportunity
is a new way of dealing with one another.

It becomes a reality
when we stop judging each other
by superficial criteria
and begin to see
and appreciate
everyone
as uniquely
talented,
capable,
and valuable.

The Land of Opportunity
is where we live and work
when we choose
to see with new eyes,
live from our hearts,
and allow ourselves
and others
to be what we truly are . . .
Ourselves.

The End

Afterword

. . . and what of the Land of Penguins?

Their story continues to unfold every day
in corporations and organizations
across the country . . .

BJ Hateley

BJ Hateley is in many ways like the lead character in this fable — colorful and extravagant, noisy and messy — a bird who is difficult to ignore. She is a free spirit who loves her work — a child of the 60's, who sees her mission in life as "comforting the afflicted, and afflicting the comfortable" (a line she once heard in a good sermon). She does both of them very well — especially the latter. She is a human potential missionary who hangs out in corporations and other organizations, showing people how they can do well by doing good.

Her USC doctoral studies in Social Ethics equipped her to be a professional do-gooder, while her years in the business world taught her to speak the language of the bottom line. She considers herself to be a pragmatic idealist. Her undergraduate training in the social sciences taught her to observe, listen, ask good questions, and analyze human behavior in all its complexity and paradoxes — great preparation for a life in business!

BJ was reluctant to leave the academic nest (she wanted to be a professor when she grew up), and spent seven years on the staff at USC — her last position there was Director of Staff Training and Professional Development. While she was supposed to be writing her dissertation she published a pop psychology/pop religion book called *Telling Your Story, Exploring Your Faith* (it paid better and was more fun).

She finally decided to try her wings in the "real world" of business, and landed at *The Los Angeles Times,* where she spent almost five years as the Manager of Training and Development. It was at the newspaper that she developed a keen interest in studying other types of "birds," and she learned a lot while directing training programs and consulting projects for the company. She left *The Times* in 1991 to form her own consulting and training company, Steps to Success.

113

Like any good peacock, BJ loves an audience, and is a popular workshop leader and public speaker. She really shows her true colors when she's talking about some of her favorite subjects: workforce diversity, leadership skills and success strategies for women, motivation, communication, sexual harassment, management development, and her all-time favorite — how to manage your boss! She also consults with organizations on other human resource issues — teambuilding, employee surveys, strategic planning, etc. She has managed to put on her penguin suit often enough to work with many respectable corporate and nonprofit clients, ranging from the Chrysler Corporation and Southern California Edison to the American Press Institute, Planned Parenthood, and the American Lung Association.

This irridescent and irrepressible bird is a Southern California native, and is one of the rare people who really loves L.A. She is the proud mom to Michael, a soon-to-be-famous young rock star (what else would you expect in L.A.?) Her favorite song is "I Gotta Be Me."

BJ Hateley can be contacted at:
"Peacock Headquarters," c/o Steps to Success,
701 Danforth Drive, Los Angeles, California 90065.

Warren H. Schmidt

Warren Schmidt looks like a penguin and likes to think of himself as a peacock. He's really quite advanced in years ("chronologically gifted" he calls it) but has six grandchildren who force him to keep playing basketball, baseball, and tennis as if he were only middle-aged.

In his long career Warren has played many roles — from minister to psychologist, from professor to city commissioner, from researcher to screen writer. He has taught others how to do Life Planning, but his own career has been shaped by a lot of unexpected opportunities — leading him from Detroit, Michigan (where he was born), to Missouri, to New York, to Massachusetts, to Ohio, to Washington, D.C. — and finally to settle down in the San Fernando Valley in California with his family of one wife (Reggie) and four kids (now increased to a clan of sixteen). While in California he has taught at two of that state's great educational institutions, UCLA and USC. Even when he "settled down" at UCLA, however, he didn't stay with a single role, moving from the psychology department to the Graduate School of Management, where he ended up as dean of executive education. After twenty two years, however, Warren finally became a mature, dependable professor of public administration at the University of Southern California (but not quite a penguin, he insists!)

Warren likes to write — particularly with someone else. He first tasted the fun of collaboration when he and Bob Tannenbaum wrote an article on "How to Choose a Leadership Pattern" for the *Harvard Business Review* — a management classic that has sold more than one million reprints. He has written books on teamwork with Gordon Lippitt and Paul Buchanan, monographs on managerial values with Barry Posner, and most recently, two books on Total Quality Management with Jerry Finnigan of the Xerox Corporation: *The Race Without a Finish Line* and *TQManager.* When BJ Hateley and Warren teamed up to write this Peacock tale, it began another delightful creative partnership that became even more interesting when Sam Weiss got into the act!

A major dimension was added to Warren's life in 1969 when he wrote a parable about divisiveness in America titled "Is It Always Right to Be Right?" Its appearance in *The Los Angeles Times* attracted the attention of four film producers (as well as Ted Kennedy and Spiro Agnew). Steven Bosustow (of Mr. Magoo fame) made an animated film of the parable; Orson Welles narrated it — and it won an Academy

Award in 1971. As an "instant expert" on films, Warren was invited to become an advisor for CRM Films — and has never stopped writing and advising. His most recent video is *The Race Without a Finish Line,* and he is now at work with BJ and Sam on an animated video of *A Peacock in the Land of Penguins.*

Warren teaches an occasional course at USC and continues to speak, consult, and conduct seminars through his little company, Chrysalis, Inc., 9238 Petit Avenue, Northridge, California 91343.

Sam Weiss

Sam is a distinguished dropout of both the Rhode Island School of Design and the Art Center College of Design. Their deans tried to convince him to stay and finish school, but his calling was elsewhere — he had pictures to draw and films to make.

He brings a unique artistic style to the illustration of books and other print materials, adding a charm all his own. With the touch of a pen, characters come to life — with the stroke of a paintbrush, whole worlds begin to unfold. In addition to being a versatile artist, he is also a musician, film director, script writer, and all-round creative spirit.

Sam is probably best known as one of the preeminent directors in the animation industry. He has written and/or directed numerous business-oriented training videos, including *The Winds of Change, To Try Again and Succeed, That's Not My Problem,* and *I Told Them Exactly How To Do It.* His most recent production is *The Race Without a Finish Line,* and he is currently directing the film adaptation of *A Peacock in the Land of Penguins.*

The films he has directed have been honored all over the world, including an Academy Award nomination for *The Legend of John Henry,* sung by

Roberta Flack with music by Herbie Hancock, and a Television Academy Emmy for *The Wrong Way Kid* (which included four adapted children's books). He has won the Gold Award of the Art Directors Club of New York, Outstanding Film of the Year at the London Film Festival, First Prize at Zagreb International Film Festival, the Jack London Award, and numerous other awards and honors.

Sam Weiss began his career as Art Director and Designer on the *Mr. Magoo* and *Bullwinkle shows*, and within a few years was directing one of the hottest animated series of the late 60's, *Hot Wheels*. He moved on to Bosustow Entertainment, where he directed more than fifty films, including four CBS one-hour specials, which required adapting thirty children's books to animation. He also produced and directed thirty-five *G.I. Joe's* for Marvel and was a Sequence Director on the critically acclaimed *Little Nemo* animated feature.

During his career he has directed the voice talents of Carol Burnett, Alan Arkin, James Earl Jones, Milton Berle, Rob Reiner, Mickey Rooney, Stan Freberg, Patrick Stewart, and other notable actors and singers.

Sam and his wonderful wife Marjorie make their home in Santa Monica, California. Requests for his autograph can be directed to: Sam Weiss Productions, 401 Sycamore Road, Santa Monica, California 90402.